An Essay in Asterisks

An Essay in Asterisks

Jena Osman

Roof Books
New York

ISBN: 0-931824-10-X
Library of Congress Catalog Card No.: 2004092271

Cover art by Luca Guerri
Author photo by Jenifer Wofford

Sections and versions of these poems have appeared in the following publications:
Bombay Gin, Conjunctions, Enough: An Anthology of Poetry and Writings Against the War, Hambone, HOW2, Issue, LIT, Pequod, Van Gogh's Ear, Verse, XCP: Cross Cultural Poetics

Roof Books are distributed by
Small Press Distribution
1341 Seventh Avenue
Berkeley, CA. 94710-1403.
Phone orders: 800-869-7553
www.spdbooks.org

This book was made possible, in part, with public funds from the New York State Council on the Arts, a state agency.

ROOF BOOKS
are published by
Segue Foundation
303 East 8th Street
New York, NY 10009
www.roofbooks.com

CONTENTS

how do you get from here to there
on an airplane
or an asterisk

AN ESSAY IN ASTERISKS

On the problem of the not-there. **REACHING INTO THE BOX AND TAKING OUT THE BAG.** If we place all stock in the space where words are missing, there is greater possibility of emotional range. Because memory is often like that as well. **LOCKING THE BOX AND PUTTING THE BAG OVER SHOULDER.** You fill in the blank (the hollow of what you can't remember) with a picture. First there is a series of images that you can't shake, as if you were there and it was a significant part of your childhood: a burning car, the crux of a tree, a desert scene and walking through the branches. Also a bright kitchen in the sun. **WALKING OUT THE DOOR AND INTO THE STREET WITHOUT LOOKING.** These must have been part of your life. Yet later you learn that they were just images from a film. Perhaps at a certain age it is difficult for a child to discern the boundaries between what is real and what is not. **RUNNING DOWN THE STREET WITH A SMALL CART.** For the child to confuse what is her experience in life and what is not. **SITTING ON THE LEDGE AND MAKING NOTES.** The moment years later, when the memories are exposed as just a piece of film is something of a shock. As if a part of life was manufactured and thus lost. **RIDING A BIKE WHILE DRINKING A DRINK.** As with the men and women in the film whose photographs are the only traces of their childhood and who then learn that their memories, based in these images, were manufactured. They were given a set of memories on which to rely. **WALKING WITH A BROOM AND SHOVEL EXTENDING BOTH ARMS.** It's all that holds them together. So that in the film, suddenly photographs no longer mean what they once did. In fact, they symbolize their inhumanity, their monstrosity. **PUSHING HAIR OUT OF THE EYES AND PLACING IT BEHIND AN EAR.** Photos are proof of our own manufacture. They shape how we recount our lives to ourselves. As does memory in its selectivity. **LIGHTING A CIGARETTE WITH A MATCH WHILE SITTING IN A CAR.** When the man remembers the event that tore them apart, it is quite different from the woman's memory of the event. And yet this event changed their lives dramatically. **WALKING SLOWLY INTO THE PARKING LOT AS IF LOST; WALKING SLOWLY BACK OUT WITH EYES LOOKING FOR SOMETHING NOT THERE.** But if just this one moment was the source of the change, how can it have been remembered so differently? They each have their own narrative for what happened, and the narratives barely touch surfaces, like two sliding metal planes one on top of the other in a kind of gear. **JUMPING UP AND DOWN STEPS IN GROUPS OF 2-3-4.** So if fact can be so swiftly undressed, what does it mean that the man is writing a book about his father? **BANGING A GRANITE SURFACE WITH BOTH PALMS AS IF IT WERE A DRUM.** In what ways will his memory manufacture the father away from himself? It is not new, this idea that memory is a creation, perhaps our most creative act, and yet it never ceases to puzzle and taunt. **TRACING THE CIRCUMFERENCE OF THE SURFACE WITH THE PALMS.** The film is frightening because of what it doesn't show and so we must place there what is only implied: our manufactured imaginings. Some are more successful at filling in the blanks than others. **CARRYING A BOY ON SHOULDERS AND THEN PULLING HIM DOWN.** Those with fewer stored images to insert in the hollow, feel that the film was over-rated. Those who are expert manufacturers, hold onto those images for days and shudder. **TRAVELING ON SHOULDERS OF THE FATHER, THEN SHRIEKING WHEN PULLED DOWN.** When you step onto the bus, there are newspapers stuffed into the money slot. The driver says "keep your money." A slot, a malfunctioning blank calling attention to itself. **HOLDING THE PALM OUTWARD TO REVEAL A RED CIRCLE PAINTED INSIDE.** Perhaps this is literalism, an economics of naturalism, a call to stop placing faith in what is representational. **STANDING FOR NATIONAL ANTHEMS.** The photo is taken of the statue straight on. And then another photo is taken of where the gaze of the statue falls. **A BOAT GOES BY WITH SAIL EXTENDED.** In its sight-line is a wall. A stone wall covered in writing. The photograph of a stone wall covered in writing. A hand holding a photograph of a stone wall covered in writing.

PRESS SCRUTINY: THE DOUBLES

*The theory of double-meaning asserts that
communication is necessary because language
is equivocal, and possible because we 'pretend'
it is univocal.*
　　　　　　　　—Sue Curry Jansen, *Censorship: The Knot that
　　　　　　　　Binds Power to Knowledge*

FIRST
An article in *The New Yorker* by Amitav Ghosh, August 12, 1996,
describes two Burmese magazine covers censored by the Press Scrutiny
Board because they are considered politically subversive. One depicts a
penguin on an ice floe and the other, a woman sitting under a tree with
falling flowers.

PENGUIN ON ICE FLOE=AUNG SAN SUI KYI

WHISPERING DOWN THE LAME
and then the man says another thing　　when he said "shoe"　　did he
really mean "you"?　　there's the problem of erratum　　when he said
"shoe"　　did he really mean "show"?　　there's a voice behind each
error　　displaying the natural talent that lies within each word　　no
matter how small　　"gotta dance!"　　"gotta ant"　　"go tan"　　"go
on"　　"Bhutan"　　did you really say that?　　did I hear you correctly?
were you talking to me?　　were you talking to me when you used the
word "hospitality"?

"SHOE"=BHUTAN
"HOSPITALITY"=THE END OF LOVE

HEARSAY

The guards arrive at the house early in the morning. They reach in and pull out all of the grandfather's poems. They find the double: climbing a mountain is a design against great leaders. Dark is one faction, light another. Use these adjectives at your own parallel. "It" is dark. The light is white. Climbing in the dark toward dawn as the white light erupts onto the eye through the dark. Darkness overtakes me, surrounds me, enlivens me. The students notice that in the story, typical connotations of dark and light begin to slip and exchange. She wears sunglasses everywhere, so as to protect her eyes from the light. Protecting one faction from the other. A design against leaders.

CLIMBING A MOUNTAIN=A DESIGN AGAINST LEADERS

HOSPITALITY

the act of being hospitable or a tendency toward being hospitable this is a triple blow to the chin   welcoming and generous behavior toward guests or strangers   jab the left hand to the chin   an instance of this   shift the weight to the right leg   cordial and generous reception of or disposition toward guests   and follow with a hard left hook to the chin   an instance of such treatment   rock the weight forward to the left leg   Middle English hospitalite   and drive a straight right to the chin   from Old French   now switch so that the last blow of the combination   from Latin hospitalitas   (stem hospitalitat)   from hospitalis   will be an uppercut to the body   of a guest   see hospital   see hospital   fling the left hand forward and upward   his offer of hospitality crushed her   in front of the opponent's face   sometimes words known for their kindness   twist the body to the left   can be a slip   after jabbing several times   a chapter of misunderstandings   the rhythm is one—one-two!   of over-reading

CHIN=THERE IS NOTHING

12

THE ENCYCLOPEDIA
. . . cheerful lively saltwater tears
willow leaves the mouth and the women
beech tree Denmark
onion revelation
have a high degree of
Ophelia:

> willow is forsaken love
> nettle is pain
> daisies are "day's eyes" are innocence
> violets are chastity, and untimely death
> poppy is death
> the forget-me-not is "don't forget Ophelia"

OPHELIA=FALLING FLOWERS

THE DOUBLE LIFE
Enter into it. The man knows the parameters of his world, its components
and how they are controlled. But one day, perhaps out of boredom, he
introduces a subversive element: an addiction, an affair, a secret business.
And at this point, every bit of his life's text is accompanied by a subtext.
For some, this double living is an excitement. But for others it is a
plague. When the man dies, his children and wife discover that he had
[an illegitimate child][an unsavory business deal][a terrible disease]. The
stable picture which propelled them through their day-to-day existence is
shattered. Now, nothing can be trusted. The children learn that the mother
held a similarly ominous secret. The mother learns that the children are
not her own. The man falls to earth and disguises himself with contact
lenses. We all suspect that something is wrong, he doesn't look like he's
from these parts. So life continues toward that inevitable moment of
revelation and shriek. You think it's your body, but in fact it's simply
being used as a container for another. At any moment your teacher can
forget to put in his lenses and turn on you. It's happened several times
before. What's your real name?

IMMEDIATE FAMILY MEMBER OR CLOSE FRIEND OR SPOUSE=ALIEN

HOSPITALITY

the knuckles are up   merely relaxes   jab at the mark   position of
guard   knuckle side up   thumb side in   waist pivot   power is
obtained   forward advance   position of guard   flicker jab
speed jab   slapped down to the target   nullify attack   the only
true lead blow   parrying, stopping, slipping   cuffing the quick shift
the step back   covering, folding, rolling, weaving   the snap away
contusion nerves, and bone   using the arms as levers   analysis of
the straight right

ARMS=SEMAPHORE SYSTEM=SOS

POSSIBILITY

the shackles tar stop   clearly syntaxes   grab at the spark   transition of
shard   shackle glide stop   dumb glide tin   taste rivet   sour is
sustained   toward a trance   transition of hard   sticker grab
deed grab   trapped round to the market   liquefy shack   the lonely
blue greed dough   tarrying, mopping, tipping   bluffing the sick rift
the depth rack   discovering, holding, polling, grieving   the trap day
confusion swerves, and lone   choosing the alarms as endeavors   synthesis
of the late night

ALARMS=METAPHOR MISSED HIM=ESSO ESS

THE DOUBLE LIFE

The man is on his knees before an oil rig, watching as his friend gets dragged away. You see the sun pushing against the horizon and the man is a shadow, watching his friend. They take the friend by his arms and he shouts an inaudible explanation. He did something wrong in his other life.

One minute the man is carried away by love. He thinks of the woman throughout the day. He says "what will I do without you?" Once he is without her, he forgets the person he was and becomes another. As this other man, he works all day trying not to think. The oil rig. There's a part of himself not there, that thought occasionally comes to mind. Is there a missing part? A vocabulary word that he used to know and now does not? He splashes water on the back of his neck to keep cool. Although he eats the same thing every day, sometimes he is one man, and sometimes he is another. As either one, he does not feel threatened by the other. In fact, he sees no apparent split. In his mind, he is complete.

MAN ON OIL RIG=CONCERT PIANIST

That is not my son, he says. And yet, he continues to stare. The clothes make the man, he remembers to think.

D+RAGS

The clothes make the man   d is for demolish   make the woman the
man   the man the woman   d is for diminish   and so they are the
same   is for dowry   but perform that sameness with a difference
for difference   at the masquerade ball, all the party goers attempt to
escape the plague   d is for devastation   of sameness   devastation
is different   repeating themselves does not help   d is for darling
take a situation and write it in code to escape the danger of articulation
is for dapper   this might provide an important service   d is for dandy
but can taking a subaltern position and dressing it up   d is for
dress-up   in new clothes   damask   (make the woman the man)
is for diamonds   perform a disservice?   d is a one way ticket to
Camden, New Jersey   the original position is still erased   is a one
way ticket to Fresno   only able to exist in someone else's clothes
is a one way ticket to Milan   although it may point effectively
a ticket to nowhere   to how clothes are constructed   d is for dry
cleaning ticket   it does not work to communicate the silenced   d is
a drag   sense is acquired by creating analogies ("samenesses")
d is for dog   links constructed by the mind which suppress meaning
to varying degrees   works like a dog   (a penguin on an ice floe)
when this construction project   d is for danger, falling rock   is
exposed as the artifice that it is   d is for the open door

D=OPEN DOOR

MODERN SCIENCE

The students studied the phrase "sexual reproduction"   Pale students
of unhallowed arts   What do I know of these . . .?   For a long time,
reproduction was thought to be a duplication of parents' attributes
From my clay to mould me   There is the scientist who creates another
man out of the parts of other men   But even after it was proven that
we are not two sets of attributes averaged into one—   The hideous
phantasm of a man   The man, a scientist, who with the help of
chemistry becomes another man   That the process is actually one of
genetic choices—   Mock the mechanism   There is the man, not
necessarily a scientist, but one who has been bitten, who changes into
an animal   The term "reproduction" was still applied   Hideous
corpse, cradle of life   What do I know about science?   (A lexical
indicator of the urge toward sameness?)   He opens his eyes; behold
I'm just a copyist   New knowledge is not immediately
accommodated lexically   The horrid thing stands at the bedside
Upsetting the laws of equivalency

In our remove, be thou at full ourself.
(Measure for Measure, 1.1.43)
ONE + ONE=ONE. Substitute one for one, then multiply by
itself. Divide by its replica so that the larger portion of one is in
fact itself. Do you recognize your progeny? ONE—ONE-TWO!
Yes, that jaw. Yes, that chin. The royal one is now the religious
one. The underling is now the royal one. The chaste one is
replaced by the spurned one. The drunk one is now the sen-
tenced one.

17

THE ENCYCLOPEDIA

. . . is hard work
bricks and mortar require a double-reading
of nut and fruit paste
chins: there is nothing
palm leaves are the spine
and the written characters are almost circular
pineapple is hospitality
the end of love
at the time of Kublai Khan
later there arose the kingdom of Ava in the north
and the kingdom of Pegu in the south
the ironic lemon is the heart
bitter rivals whose wars carried on for centuries
the singular voice, mourning.
an antidote to enchantment
the discourse of the moth

AUTOBIOGRAPHY

study the phrase
pale students
duplication of thought
moulds me
creates another man
out of the parts of other men
with chemistry I become
one who has been
bitten
an animal
a corpse
I know about sameness
I'm a copyist
not immediately horrid
but a thing of equivalency

ERRANT AIR
AIR • HEIR • ERE • ERR

We move from the middle, what's in the air?
color, odor, taste, gas,
mixed in the main of night O! gentle and gentle
an ox with less amour is arguably carpe diem,
ox • on • um,
the other guys in the atmosphere
were ancient though on top of things
four men in the sky, firm like space over the round
public expression of utter penury

I want to   feel time slowing
        I want to   feel it   slowing
                    so I can read   the pauses

in the above, PAUSE means
a) air   c) heir
b) ere   d) err

the blank rests in the pause so that the listener must fill it in
choice is not a blank
"I've made my choices"
not a blank

characters impress with their auras
the personal appearance or overbearing manner:
overbearing man-heir
of our affectations.

a • b • c • d

In music, it's a melody,
our tune, our support of terrible parts in a granite position.
a sole forage choice, our instrument.
Arch breath. Clear,

in • on • take • up
and walk a space between the pauses

SPACE means
a) air   c) heir
b) ere   d) err

an exposé on towers or warning against order
tawdry, school lore frisson,
vent late, ax.

(air? err?)

Together pebbles lick an utter circle and vent (late)(ax).
bled of sensation of seven (acts)
originals • atoms • spheres:

>   *Mid-life Anguish air, aye from Old Men are in Latin or from*
>   *Greek aire.*
>   *Banner appears: fresh French air from old Fresh ire from Latin*
>   *anger and area.*
>   *Melodic battalion aria.*
>   *In Anguish please sense apples contracted intricately.*

A certain who
merits or
is titled by law
or by the terminals of will

to merit the states of another.
A certain who
proceeds or is
in a mine of seeds
the legal run • idle • preface.

One who is idle or guarded—
an idol to my reservoir,

a mortgage of my ideas—
thus becomes a possessor, a scissor.

arch • precious who • for soon I'd rather be

a mirror or stake • be ink.

inside the pause
vying for late receptors
more as standards
in arches.

to ghost away.

> . . . *one of the motorcyclists was waving a bamboo*
> *stake on which was impaled the head of a young man.*
>   *"Allahu akbar!" the motorcyclists shouted, waving*
> *their sickles in celebration at having killed a man they*
> *regarded as a sorcerer.**

---

* Nicholas D. Kristof, "Fears of Sorcerers Spur Killings in Java," *New York Times*,
Tuesday, October 20, 1998, front page.

GHOST means
a) lair   c) hierarchy
b) here   d) terror

Much Anguish in Old Fresh horror from Latin mirror. *

PUNS=DANGER

* The trick of words to be themselves and another simultaneously is often labeled "homophonic." Some writers consider sound to be the lift toward translation, when in fact something much more subversive is going on. The words prove themselves to be double-agents. Each word maintains its disquieting doppelganger, sometimes visible (and therefore noted by our dictionaries), sometimes successfully undercover. For example: "The word was fêted in France" and "The word was fetid in France." Typographical mistakes sometimes reveal the double that lays low. Certain governments spend their time trying to uncover them. As if there was code there.

BOWDLERIZER

> *I have carefully plugged at the words which hurt. The
> book wears quite a new aspect . . .*
> — Stephen Crane on revising *Maggie, Girl
> of the Streets* at the request of his publisher

don't talk about soldiers killing wolves
the wolf is in the box

```
┌─────────────┐
│  WOLF       │
│             │
└─────────────┘
```

what is the wolf   who is the wolf
is the wolf made of wool   wouldn't you woo the wolf if you will
what is the will of the wolf
to kill the soldier?

the invisible frame is sleep or sheep

```
┌─────────────┐
│  DAISY      │
│             │
└─────────────┘
```

deported for not playing the star spangled banner

suppress the s for spelling sex

omeo and liet

war garden

and grass

killed   glass

fixation on steel
sparrow disdain
beat any metal object
drop dead from exhaustion

                              take all the grass from the lawns
attack flowers and grass

their self indictment
and pulverized spectacles

cutting their long hair,
or breaking their semi-high-heeled shoes

A gentleman wears a bow(d)ler hat in the company of ladies.

A man wears a bow in the company of lads.

A gentle we, a bowler hat, the company of ladies.

Man, we bowl at the company.

A gentleman wears a bow in company.

Gentle hat of ladies.

A gentle(d)man wear(d)s a bow(d)ler ha(d)t in the comp(d)any of lad(d)ies.

WOLF

sexual insult for sexual assault
loving-hearted for loosely hung
she for he
she for he
laymen for ministers

fade-outs become dissolves

PATIO

patios for bedrooms
dancers for prostitutes
native for black
nylon pocketbook for pig's ear

LOVE

"Till love came and told me I shouldn't sleep" for
        "until I could sleep where I shouldn't sleep"
"I've tried most of the other rooms" for
        "I've tried all of the other rooms"
"I've heard of perfume from Spain" for
        "I get no kick from cocaine"
"We are all three skeptics, scoffers at all normal ties" for
        "we are all three infidels who scoff at our marriage ties"

26

wife for woman
imaginary disease for venereal disease
wanton for whore
insides for entrails
bat for rat
poison for arsenic
almonds! for nuts!

denying the enemy an infrastructure for bombing targets in cities
soft targets for people
laying down a carpet for saturation bombing
daisy cutters for 15,000 pound bombs that explode just above
        the ground

DROPPING LEAFLETS

Help me come up with a strategy to get through this
white noise.
—U.S. Representative Cynthia McKinney,
November 2001

Are we on the ground now? Ally cells and I said operations.
We cleared 50% of a wonderful friend and enduring opposition.
Take the solid.
Louder.
We clearly are loud. We are the postal system.
No evidence has been information.
Attacking the caves. Are you on the ground enduring?
A wonderful friend ramped it up.
You ought to open your mail.
Opposition element: the air. The talents work with precision.
84%. The population attacking the caves, the talents work with the
caves and tunnels.
Hiding in caves, wavering in caves and hiding in mosques.
A wonderful friend on the ground.
Freedom I said: the enduring ally cells.
Interested in the view, in our aid sensitivities.
50% to the front of our effort adding that 80% are willing to play.
Independent oper-oppo-sition forces that are rosy.
So make assumptions on the ground. Are we on the ground now?
Scraps of information work from opposition.
Can be more than air. The target. The air liaison.
Campaign with the bombing and entirely happy.
Attacking the leaflets.
We keep working hiding in hiding in caves
and cowering in cowering in cowering in caves
and I could say confidential areas.
The mosques and rest efforts are mad.

Execution in the targeting of democracy.

Those risks culti-targeting to minimize the individual.

An obligation to the spirit of enterprise.

A war of roundup freezing worldwide, and proceeding on course.

Training facilities, proceeding on course, freezing their guided munitions.

A population is tons of struggle against evil.

A civilized world of innocents in the mud, an enemy that's on the ground for there is no neutral ever. No neutral homeland.

For the first time first time first time in history
ordinary busi-security bioterror
to defend enemies with the no-ness of life.

Confident in destruction / complete and cause / certain of the rightness of this time / in the right / man the victories / to comment for a freer world history / committee of evil / defeat the forces / we will fight and great coalition wherever they are an era of over flight right against terror basing global terror the global trade and lives of our world improve / the modern alliance / I like citizens / but rather than the dust settle it could mean / as acknowledged / the carpet bombs precision bombs / as long as 23 months and I said go to America on alert / get a softball to school if you work / take your child / game this afternoon / game or a soccer to the president's going to go to the game / the fight / our new baseball game / to help us in our task / force will sign terrorists tracking American citizens / to protect level warriors / the decibel from these shadows / open your mail louder

NOVEL OF NOWHERE

Realize public shapes and the single slide into the treasury. How she falls into conversation as a product of time passing. The listening is only for the sake of future production. In separate places, the voices seem as if talking to each other when in fact they converse in opposite cities. Silence as time passes: a distasteful deductible gift. An appeal for rice or something else that someone needs.

The wizard of ozacide.

The leader tells the others what is right and wrong. The wall markings. This is not a mentioning of one object in order to disguise another. It slips into your mouth.

Please repeat the curtain. Buildings fall into streams of light and light falls to the bottom. Streams in the street and close to the gutter. The shot is sometimes the cause. Like some shots, the last breath—that forces itself apart and falls.

The leader beaks his head between two sticks (not Bosch). The bones are beneath his foot. His men throw silver globes to hit other globes, the clicking (in separate places) barely registers in their faces. A strike is made. It must be in a flat place.

He plays cards at the long table and then, spent, lifts his wooden arms to bed. Here, also, many women in bright colors pray. They are never otherwise on their knees. It is hoped that tomorrow the whole city will warm itself in a singular act of will. Surfaces clutter us up. A patch of land festers.

First response when Bosch flew overhead was the reluctance of brown to thin itself within the green. His jacket was of neither color. A dent in the forehead. That day, the sun was full. In the event of a proper marketplace, you might see stars.

This is how I spent several years. In the flat pictures. Calling forth only the edges of the hills. The buildings sport various lights according to time of day. Memory is like hills on an edge. Three pages lost after riding uphill. Quietude in continuity (what is left and where it is left). With three brothers and a bad forecast. One hand lets itself down while the other is lifting the pail up into the black. A constellation. An urgency in seeing all the pieces in relation to the figure.

Perhaps it is the curtain falling. Suddenly a stream. The curtain falls into the stream and then down into the gutter. The curtain falls off the side of the building and slowly levitates. The city has facades, then curtains. Falling that causes the breath, a voice box booms: "It's not inevitable," then falls into the stream. Some disagree.

These disputes become deadly.
The attackers lay in ambush with automatic weapons.

It is a trial to go back to another person's home. A parquet floor leads the eye to her fingers. Exchange of objects that rest beneath. The hands exchange words for something of lesser value. Her fingers, feather fan, with one loose ring: it sits on the shelf tied to the book. Each value connected to a physical, mathematical life. Emblems grieve to form a misunderstanding.

He and she bartering their palms with battering

eyes fray, a delayed mechanical

what they say disappears

an alternative to trade

(slow face)

sets in

barter demands a desire

whoever sat upon the stool (the leader or Bosch)
somehow flooded through the wall

The light dissipates into the last provision. When you breathe quickly
this affects the light. The shot is sometimes the cause of light and
sometimes not. Like some shots, the light dissipates into its emanation—
provided there is a repetition as in the last moment of breath. See what
happens?

The men mutter and pace, grim and tense.
Soldiers patrol the rutted road.

here they are, my three brothers,
with the axes
chopping down the door

We are in the room, debris in the creases of our knees washing the
tide into the dry skin. Parts of the treasury release into the landscape
creating the unsworn parts (the country).
There is a man with a straw hat and a yoked ox. He is sleepwalking into
an abyss.

His hands gesture to her "walk light,"
"make sure they don't hear you"

There are children who threaten them.

On one side of the curtain a little man plays cards all night. On the other
side, the same thing. The division between the sides—whether the sides
are bad or good—is never clarified. All we can conclude is their burning,
how their (sur)faces seem startled
as much a response to sound as to flame

1000 people fight hand to hand.
and pelt each other with stones.

We are prepared to do little. Answers to simple questions exaggerate their loss. Pain had little effect on the picture's symmetry, the houses at desired distances. Whether you and I treat each other well in conversation is another matter. My brothers are approaching.

Certain parts of the tree are missing. Ladder, ax, Bosch looks up. Branches are for fire or stake or illicit meeting.

(later . . .)

The wings are fibrous, two and two on each side of the dead man's stretcher. Blue and yellow filled with strings inwardly. Procession under the dark tree. Robes, trains, crosses, service, resolution. Certain parts of the trees are missing.

In the particulars of her face:
orange tallow marsh-weed and dollars

wrought-iron values of dark and light
force what we see into
what we might

The hollow vine blasts an empty hand into what it holds: massacres of stamina. Not a fingerprint of planning. Chew through the border with a nail file. A handshake doesn't change things on the ground.

The brothers hide their wrongdoing with the worst coat of paint. They devise a schema with branches and bones. Their sockets cleft to the trunk.

The wings are fibrous on the men that pray and sting the foot of the bed. Cataracts of string course through them, insides too full for anything good. They are thus considered opposite of what they are made.

First the body that lies flat there, the head kept alone under the guard of two others. He has concern with what is apparent inwardly and for the wrongdoings of the body, temporary of anything good. Goodness reveals itself in a short string from the knee to the foot and up through the arm, down through a pendulum. The body is read as a message. The leader tears it up.

An increase of loss through the damage. A life engine markedly rows toward the seeming bystander. Portrayal of all that is part dull pain, part responsive quagmire. She takes care of the husband (not Bosch) and endearingly bitter, switches the course in his sleep. They elevate into the materials, past words of warning.

What is the pattern that darkens the humor of who you are? You have something in focus that you listen to and list.

They arrive as a group
levitating or riling the senses

The man risks understanding and the other man is caught behind the
 eyes
The man is caught in the art of not living and the other man controls the
 stare
The man controls the sticks of dream and the other man did gasp and
 grasp

THE ASTOUNDING COMPLEX

Opening Arguments

In his book *Frame Analysis*, Erving Goffman describes the "astounding complex" as a mystery that we think we should be able to rationally solve but can't. I think of what might fall into this category:

UFOs
fortune telling
coincidence
Bartleby the Scrivener
Odradek

We can't get to a place of solution; the astounding complex is the opposite of law. Meanwhile, as we move through the everyday, the law is not astounded by us. It reads us and comes to a final interpretation over and over again.

When we are confronted by that which astounds and astonishes, our response is a legal one. We want to question it, force it to confess its mystery, and then pass a final judgment. Through a legislative interpretive activity, we try to drive the incomplete into a comprehensible and absolute state. Unfortunately our proposed acts can only fail to become laws. We risk our re-elections.

The role of the court is to move the jury into a realm of reason that leads it beyond passion or pity. The "intoxicant" of empathy and emotion is abolished in the name of clear sight and interpretation. With a skilled application of distancing strategies, the facts/objects of the case can be established with certainty.

Sometimes that's a matter of grammar.

First Case Scenario

Summary Excerpt:
UNITED STATES v. RODRIGUEZ-MORENO
Argued December 7, 1998 — Decided March 20, 1999

A drug distributor hired respondent and others to find a New York drug dealer
who stole cocaine from him during a Texas drug transaction and to hold captive
the middleman in the transaction, Ephrain Avendano, during the search. The
group drove from Texas to New Jersey to New York to Maryland, taking
Avendano with them. Respondent took possession of a revolver in Maryland
and threatened to kill Avendano. Avendano eventually escaped and called
police, who arrested respondent and the others. Respondent was charged in a
New Jersey District Court with, inter alia, using and carrying a firearm in rela-
tion to Avendano's kidnapping, in violation of 18 U.S.C. sect. 924(c)(1). He
moved to dismiss that count, arguing that venue was proper only in Maryland,
the only place where the Government had proved he had actually used a gun.
The court denied the motion, and respondent was convicted of the sect.
923(c)(1) offense. The Third Circuit reversed. After applying what it called the
"verb test," it determined that venue was proper only in the district where a
defendant actually uses or carries a firearm.

Procedure: The Verb Test
NITE SATES (MORE Venn diagrams)

Chatter the embers, you must cut off the arc. Your action, Ephrain
Avendano, is like a knock out from the inside of the arc. You fell down
through the air of Texas New Jersey New York Maryland, into a pond;
a session held in the mind.

Ill Avendano. Avendano in the ally eluding memory. A call. New Jersey
District Court whines, hums and whistles a fire. You relocate, don't
realize your hat is still on; the hat disintegrates (morally). Government

ads target and reckon use. You injure your own feelings, extinguish them, dent and declare guilty. Concealed Circuits familiarize then ravage the "verb test," invalidate all use of spoken or written fires.

To carry on: Venn roses whine, hum and whistle expressing ire. Ions are neglected. You curse, curt, and we reckon dents. Situated off (you are off) a hen throws dice and appears cured. The United States is tough; your Third Circuit presents false information. You declare that verbs deter us from action; you are off. Your Court as ever a verb and so judges the illusion that men are required to injure themselves. Off in spite of the big bed you assume to exist during tins to din duct men. Violently torn into pieces, whine, hum and whistle—the ads are weeping; you're neglecting your kid. A rime rests with torso vertical, tin arts violently torn into pieces. Local venn ropes encircle your car (now that's art) a target you neglected. The United States chatters. Answer chatter, hat on, advance your pace. Here you mimic a coin with absurd results. Then mimic unit rime, "hi, I do no mat hat" into a pond. You employ Maryland and curse "during and in relation to" the kid's urgent pleas. Your kid, "hi," he's off and suffers. As you walk back and forth (there's art to walking), venn props present false rime. An offense to adore.

Second Case Scenario

Opinion Excerpt
VICTOR v. NEBRASKA
Argued January 18, 1994—Decided March 22, 1994

The government must prove beyond a reasonable doubt every element of a charged offense. Although this standard is an ancient and honored aspect of our criminal justice system, it defies easy explication. In these cases, we consider the constitutionality of two attempts to define "reasonable doubt."

Procedure 1: Defining Doubt
"MORAL CERTAINTY" NOT MODERN

how to define reasonable doubt,
count the ways
the prosecutors must define
for today's audience
a reasonable and prudent group
what might cause them to hesitate
during an important transaction
of life

1. have they been prevented
from experiencing their usual
"moral certainty"?
2. imagination does not lead to
reasonable doubt;
"everything relating to human affairs...
is open to imaginary doubt"
3. hesitation

does definition violate due process?
do they understand the instructions?
"We are using a formulation

that we believe will become less clear
the more we explain it."
as definition brings the familiar further
from us in a stalled moment

"I would vacate
the sentence
of death"
wrote Blackmun.

Procedure 2: No "Uncertain" Terms
HEY, RAN HE IN SINS?

        he ways

    he   sec   fine

    f r   ay's

    a reas   le an

    ha m   ca se hem   hesitate
                ham case hem hesitate
    ring an imp r an   ransac i n
                ring an imp ran ransack in
        life

    1. have hey   even

       experiencing heir

    "   er a   "?

    2. imagin   es
                imagines
      as a le   ;
                as ale
    "every hing e ing   man affairs...

    is pen   imaginary   "

    3. s   i n

fin i n vi l e   pr ess?
fin in vile press?
hey   r an he in s   i ns?
hey, ran he in sins?
"We are sing a   rm   ion
"We are sing arm ion
we   li ve will   me less clear

he m e we explain i ."

as   fin i n rings he familiar   her
as fin in rings
in a s all   men

"I   vaca t e   of   "

lack   .

Continuing Court Narrative

In Victor vs. Nebraska, the petitioner claimed that due process was violated when the phrase "reasonable doubt" (as in "guilty beyond a") was defined by the court for the jury in the following way:

a) that which would cause a reasonable and prudent person in an important transaction of life, to hesitate before taking the represented facts as true;
b) that which would prevent the jurors from feeling a "moral certainty" of the accused's guilt;
c) an actual and substantial doubt arising from evidence, rather than from the imagination

The petitioner argued that a phrase such as "moral certainty" was too malleable for today's citizen, that it was not a comprehensible instruction to the jurors. The Supreme Court ruled that due process had not been violated; however they stated that the act of defining "reasonable doubt" was not at all helpful, especially with the phrase "moral certainty" included in the definition, because for many that is a much more specific and structured measure of probability than "reasonable doubt." Whereas the petitioner had critiqued the phrase because of its invitation to multiple interpretations—its ambiguity in light of today's jury—the court critiqued the same phrase for being too definitive, precise to the point where intended meaning might have been blurred. In its majority opinion, the Supreme Court stated that although "moral evidence" is not a "mainstay of the modern lexicon," its meaning is consistent with its original 19th century meaning: the instructions were understood, the interpretation of these instructions was complete.

The law cannot afford to have its language perceived as decadent with assumptions that can be challenged. Yet trials are based on indeterminacy, demanding that a jury understand the legal issue at hand from one perspective, and then from another. The apparent seamlessness of a law which can separate out the guilty from the innocent is dependent on a continual re-framing; a jarring rhythm from one perception to another.

Third Case Scenario

Summary Excerpt:
GRAY v. MARYLAND
Argued December 8, 1997 — Decided March 9, 1998

Anthony Bell confessed to the police that he, petitioner Gray, and another man participated in the beating that caused Stacy Williams' death. After the third man died, a Maryland grand jury indicted Bell and Gray for murder, and the State tried them jointly. When the trial judge permitted the State to introduce a redacted version of Bell's confession, the detective who read it to the jury said "deleted" or "deletion" whenever the name of Gray or the third participant appeared. Immediately after that reading, however, the detective answered affirmatively when the prosecutor asked, "after [Bell] gave you that information, you subsequently were able to arrest . . . Gray; is that correct?" The State also introduced a written copy of the confession with the two names omitted, leaving in their place blanks separated by commas. The judge instructed the jury that the confession could be used as evidence only against Bell, not Gray. The jury convicted both defendants.

Procedure: Erasing Gray (Deletion as Protection)
[X] v. MXXXLXND

Anthony Bell confessed to the police thXt he, petitioneX [X] Xnd XnotheX mXn pXXticipXted in the beXtinX thXt cXused Stacy Williams' deXth. XfteX the thiXd mXn died, X Maryland XXXnd juXX indicted Bell and [X] foX muXdeX, Xnd the State tXied them jointlX. When the tXiXl judXe peXmitted the State to intXoduce X XedXcted veXsion of Bell's confession, the detective who Xead it to the juXX sXid "deleted" oX "deletion" wheneveX the nXme of [X] oX the thiXd pXXticipXnt XppeXXed. ImmediXtelX XfteX thXt XeXdinX, howeveX, the detective XnsweXed XffiXmXtivelX when the pXosecutoX Xsked, "after [Bell] gave you that information, you subsequently were able to arrest...[X]; is that correct?" The State XlsointXoduced X wXitten copX of the confession with the two nXmes omitted, leXvinX in theiX plXce blXnks sepXXXted by commXs. The judXe instXucted the juXX thXt the confession could be used Xs evidence onlX XgXinst Bell, not [X]. The juXX convicted both defendXnts.

addendum:

Emily Dickinson wrote

> Step lightly on
> This narrow spot —
> The broadest Land
> That grows
> Is not so Ample
> As the Breast
> These Emerald
> Seams enclose
>
> Step lofty, for
> This name be told
> As far as Cannon
> Dwell
> Or Flag subsist
> Or Fame export
> Her deathless
> Syllable

But in the fasicle version, this poem appears as a field of X's, due to how Dickinson chose to cross her T's and F's:

```
S X e p   l i g h x l y    on
X his   n a r r o w    S p o x —
X h e   b r o a d e s x   X a n d
T h a t   g r o w s
I s     n o X  s o   a m p l e
A s   X h e   B r e a s x
X h e s e    E m e r a l d
S e a m s   e n c l o s e .


S X e p   l o f t y , f o r
X h i s   n a m e   b e xold
A s   f a r  a s  C a nnon
D w e l l
O r   X l  a g   S u b s i s X
O r   X a m e  E x p o r X
H e r     d e a x h l e s s
S y l l a  b l e
```

The X's are stitches in the picture of the poem. Letters are actually what sew the "seam," and what they enclose is the dead body in its emerald "spot." What is equally interesting is the apparent discarding of the dash. Thus, the poem has a squarer look to it—a plain, a plot, a field. The more defined/geometric the space, the more it resembles a space enclosed. The dashes signify an opening, but this poem has a concrete and pictorial surface, patched in places by the letter "X." *

There's a confession that links a man's name to a body beneath a field of X's. The man attempts to remove his name from the penalty box. He wants to become the X, the blank spot. The court eventually agrees to this, but the mark is still there. The X is both an absence and a presence.

---

* "The abstract term 'equality' took on materiality as we moved towards the church hall polling station and the simple act, the drawing of an X, that ended over three centuries of privilege for some, deprivation of human dignity for others. [. . .]A strange moment: the first time man scratched the mark of his identity, the conscious proof of his existence, on a stone must have been rather like this." (Nadine Gordimer, "Standing in the Queue")

Literaturizing the Problem

Shakespeare's *Measure for Measure* portrays the justice system as a form of apparel that can be put on and taken off. In other words, a process of substitution. In 1984 I saw a Royal Shakespeare production of this play which began with the image of the Duke, his back to the audience, looking intently into a full-length mirror. His arms were stretched out to the sides and his long velvet robe framed his body. Soon after this mirrored glance, he passed on his robes (and responsibilities) to his deputy, Angelo.

He says "In our remove, be thou at full ourself."

Measure for Measure enacts the complicated claims of stable objectivity made by judicial language. When Isabella tries to appeal her brother's sentence of death for pre-marital sex, Angelo replies "it is the law, not I, that condemns." Angelo's struggle to prove that the law is free from any arbitrary or subjective source is almost instantly destroyed when his position as lawmaker collides with his personal desire for Isabella. And by the end of the play, not only are the laws masked by a veil of objectivity and truth, but so are the *subjects* of the law: Claudio gets a substitute to suffer his sentence in his name, and Isabella similarly gets a substitute to endure her deflowering. On the surface it seems the law will be carried out appropriately; underneath the surface are characters who defy the law's interpretation/reading of them. And the originator of all this masking—the Duke—is masked himself under the hood of a monk's robe, having escaped the law's reading of him as lawmaker by using Angelo as a substitute.

The characters, unable to give in to such objectification have created a frozen exterior that shields a fluid and changeable interior, almost unapproachable by the interpretive act. They harbor a complex set of astounding complexes beneath their seemingly knowable exteriors. The play's form itself performs the problem: on the surface it appears to be a comedy—it has the traditional happy ending of a big wedding to prove it. However, it seems almost incomprehensible that Isabella, after making such a powerful case against saving her brother's life with a gift of her virginity to Angelo, should suddenly be so willing to marry the not-so-heroic Duke. Because of such inexplicable contradictions, *Measure for Measure* is often referred to as a "problem play."

Fourth Case Scenario

Summary Excerpt:
BROGAN v. UNITED STATES
Argued December 2, 1997 — Decided January 26, 1998

Petitioner falsely answered "no" when federal agents asked him whether he had received any cash or gifts from a company whose employees were represented by the union in which he was an officer. He was indicted on federal bribery charges and for making a false statement within the jurisdiction of a federal agency in violation of 18 U.S.C. Sect. 1001. A jury in the District Court found him guilty. The Second Circuit affirmed, categorically rejecting his request to adopt the so-called "exculpatory no" doctrine, which excludes from Sect. 1001's scope false statements that consist of the mere denial of wrongdoing.

Procedure: The Exculpatory No (Antonyms as Denial)
BAN NITE SATES

Large true question "no"
dog tame dame as goodbye
dry give away an ash
its pot pipe plays
I'm absent she
goodbye as water.
as no dice
tame neck uncooked or queen wine city
with her slurred speech
tame youth trumpet 18 U.S.C. Sect. 1001.
Her District Court penniless goodbye crown.
Her Second Circuit flaccid, countless welcome is not searchless
opt-out her uncalled-for "exculpatory no"
doesn't dine, goodbye
keeps in Sect. 1001 unable to cope
wine city sock
free her after kitchen rights.

Letting go: his everything
body unable or wine city free
excessive "exculpatory no."
Soprano any Court Appeals
indecision loosens her "exculpatory no"
doesn't dine, with lots of help and painless youth.
It's eternal, begins "any" wine city—shock, wine city "of whatever
kind,"
United States v. Gonzales, lungless she
you
she
"no" doesn't rest, doesn't search.
Large good health
socks do some inches
gulp kitchens
crown leaves to no stake cakes:
sock her city builds on pipe
and cities' socks "pervert governmental functions,"
a sock gulps kitchens and crowns yes.
United States Gilliland soothes,
is not a bought sock
red illiterate
early her "spirit" her Fifth Amendment welcomed
acid her Fifth Amendment does everyone just great.
E.g., United States Apfelbaum, 445 U.S. doesn't begin to placate
sock her "exculpatory no"
doesn't dine with many singles
her taking is sock health without using unenthusiastic thorns
queen "pile on" on yes with help
her blurring grip, an odd, undressed Congress.

Final Questions

Your verdict must be based solely and exclusively on the evidence in the case. You may not be governed by passion, prejudice, sympathy, or any motive whatsoever except a fair and impartial consideration of the evidence.

In other words, don't tamper with the grammar.

If facts are empty masks
or velvet robes

Must we give ourselves over to an astounding belief in completion

Or can a new grammar of decision
defy execution[*]

And propose more useful scenarios

[*] "The Supreme Court will hear the case of Daryl Atkins, a Virginia death row inmate with mental retardation, to consider whether executing those with mental retardation offends society's 'evolving standards of decency' and thus violates the Eighth Amendment's ban on cruel and unusual punishment" (Associated Press, 9/25/01).

Summaries
EARLS OF SALISBURY, NORTHHAMPTON AND NOTTINGHAM v. GARNET
Argued: 1606

Garnet, a Catholic priest learned through Catesby about the Gunpowder Plot. It was understood that if the plot was ever discovered, Garnet could reveal the truth. After the plot was discovered, Garnet was arrested. At his trial he truthfully told the details that he knew and was then executed at the west end of Old St. Paul's, 3 May, 1606. Garnet was author of a scholarly treatise on the art of equivocation.

and

UNITED STATES v. NIXON
Argued: 1974

The District Court, upon the motion of the special prosecutor, issued a subpoena to the president requiring him to produce certain tapes and documents relating to precisely identified meetings between the president and others. President Nixon released edited transcripts of some of the subpoenaed conversations, but his counsel filed a "special appearance" and moved to quash the subpoena on the grounds of executive privilege. The Burger court stated that he must yield to the need for that evidence. Jaworski was special prosecutor. Nixon was represented by James St. Clair. Rehnquist, then a junior member, excused himself from this case because he had been a former aide to Watergate defendant John Mitchell.

Procedure: Duel of Equivocations

Garnet: I am bound to keepe the secrets of confession, and to disclose nothing that I heard in Sacramentall confession.

Earle of Nottingham: If one confessed this day to you that to morrow morning he meant to kill the King with a dagger; must you conceal it?

Garnet: I must conceal it.[*]

Marshall: What, in any of these tapes, is involved in the impeachment proceedings?

Jaworski: What it really narrows down to is a somewhat simple but very important issue in the administration of criminal justice. And that is whether the president, in a pending prosecution, can withhold material evidence from the court, merely on his assertion that the evidence involves confidential communications.

Earle of Salisbury: I desire the libertie of you to aske you some questions of the nature of Confessions?

Garnet: You may my lord, and I will answer you as well as I can.

Marshall: What, in any of these tapes, is involved in the impeachment proceedings?

Earle of Salisbury: . . . there needs no secrecie. . . . He professed no penitencie, and therefore you could not absolve him.

---

[*] "A Bronx man was freed from prison yesterday by a federal judge who said that he never would have been convicted of murder if the jury had known 13 years ago that a guilt-racked teenager had admitted committing the crime to a priest . . ." (*New York Times*, 7/25/01, page 1).

[*To this Garnet denyed to answere, by which the hearers might see his mind.*]

Justice Marshall: Slightly judicial.

St. Clair: Entirely judicial.

Marshall: And that's what's before us?

St. Clair: And that we moved to quash.

Marshall: What, in any of these tapes, is involved in the impeachment proceedings?

Garnet, *faintly*: I might not disclose it to any, because it is a matter of secret confession and would endanger the life of divers men.

Burger: The very integrity of the judicial system and public confidence in the system depend on full disclosure of all the facts within the framework of the rules of evidence.

Earle of Northampton: The matter of Confession, which before you refused to confesse, because you would save lives, you confessed it now to endanger your owne life, and therefore your former answere was idle and frivolous.

St. Clair: My learned brother has approached this case, I think, in a traditional point of view . . .

Earle of Nottingham: If one confessed this day to you that to morrow morning he meant to kill the King with a dagger; must you conceal it?

Garnet: I might not disclose it to any, because it was matter of secret confession and would endanger the life of divers men.

Jaworski: Now the president may be right in how he reads the Constitution. But he may also be wrong. And if he is wrong, who is there to tell him so? If he is the sole judge, and he is in error in his interpretation, then he goes on being in error in his interpretation.

Justice Stewart: Well, then this Court will tell him so. That's what this case is about, isn't it?

Jaworski: Well, that's what I think the case is about, yes, sir.

BOXING CAPTIONS

> *I wanted to respond to the simple gesture of the figures
> . . . without pathos, without dramatic movement,
> without telling stories! For the painter or sculptor,
> simple acts of the human figure, such as inclining the
> head, raising an arm, gesturing with the hand, moving
> a leg, provide such an expressive richness that themes
> such as standing, coming, going, turning, and the like
> would suffice to occupy an artist's lifetime.*
> —Oskar Schlemmer

Simple acts: The theater is ranging across the boundaries of its materials.
I find myself through a device, a synthesizer of discrete emblems,
disconnected on summation and realized in the limits of time zone
and national sphere. I'm a figure mechanized by its last potentials and
careful of new hypotheses. Emblems run their course through me, serve
to engender fantasies, the image conditioned to promise change, to
approach us but not too closely.

FIGURE ONE
*Force the opponent's left and lead to the right
with the left glove.*

FIGURE TWO
*Step forward and left, at the same time drive
a straight right to the chin.*

FIGURE THREE
*The left hand, after executing the parry, is in
a position of block ready for opponent's right.*

Fig. 6.

Stage realm is ranging through these gestures. What popular thing directing their geography, realized in the limits of a romantic confrontation, animated as the antique need for today and the loss of self one feels in the market place. The term mummery appears like a light: a moral variety, a diagram in the vaudeville

FIGURE FOUR
noh hearing, noh voting, my soldier will know
men leer strands of century
then linger on woe

FIGURE FIVE
on top of the right gun
a layer of guy
a stance over madder
victorious in light

Fig. 15.

FIGURE SIX
Race on and tongue tie   on sounds in a bay
Get a word   clean and dry

History from materials wades cautiously into a contentious debate. The history of reflection: "I am the votes." An actor of naturalness, then helicopters churn overhead. The government blinked. This sculptor crafts a spiritual artifice while thousands cheer wildly in the arena built for the role. We will examine the changes caused by the longest war.

FIGURE SEVEN
Abhorrence

FIGURE EIGHT
Self Abasement

FIGURE NINE
Utter Abandonment

Fig. 24.

Emblems disconnect making dozens of arrests. The absurd hand broke up a drug ring, the result of new mechanization. They also seized 18 firearms, our sphere of life aided by corrupt employees. A suspicious package was reported, our recognition is loaded, is mechanized. It would be met by another vehicle, our time to create. Workers count ballots, technology and fantasies, then succeed in ousting one sign.

FIGURE TEN
National Election commission workers count
ballots for the National Assembly.

FIGURE ELEVEN
A former intelligence officer is being held in a
prison.

FIGURE TWELVE
Life goes on at a café while protesters march by.

Fig. 33.

Taken between things, we clear the final state hurdle. It is really natural to approve a compromise bill that runs through me. What popular thing is suspended from school, passive at its scaffold. No charges are likely to be filed; they are animate as the market place. We discuss shooting and stabbing—the mummery, seen as a lie. After taking her to the woods, diagrams step up their assault, that is, shape the world. No sound as we try to decide whether to sign a physical—an optical—event and hold direct talks with its composer (who fails to defeat the rebels). Sounds out of the body are the form of two who approve a plan to place you under house arrest, complete with distribution and precision and fear that you might try to escape.

FIGURE THIRTEEN
*Every object is naturally drawn to the
earth's center.*

FIGURE FOURTEEN
*Another was given credit for that, which
prevented the former from saying such a
thing out loud.*

FIGURE FIFTEEN
*Then he decided to measure humidity with
a ball of cotton.*

Fig. 42.

Independence and time threatened to freeze his assets. His material,
however—the words for which he was arrested—an improvised existence
as they unfurled banners of protest. Alone they're free in circumstance,
renouncing his ties. He is material for higher potential and the conflict
ends. Reproduction for the latter brings a halt to spring, detached limitations
decked out in new riot gear. Humans are certain to be listening, opening
markets to competition. Depth extensions can wipe out linear form, leaving
workers without jobs. Rigid geometry of space enjoys expanded export,
runs right through me, driving unions to lock arms.

FIGURE SIXTEEN
*Smith was freed on grounds of prosecutorial
misconduct.*

FIGURE SEVENTEEN
*Eleanor Reese shows damage to the trunk of
the car that was removed from behind her house.*

FIGURE EIGHTEEN
*Ivory V. Nelson has tackled difficult problems
at universities.*

Fig. 51.

Manifestations of nothingness hold meetings willing to listen to values they fulfilled. Simple acts: The living means of representation help people in poor countries, their flesh and measure integrating into the world emblem economy. They are not equilibrium under siege. The stability of a deficiency is mechanized, scheduled to culminate through borrowed tactics. Transient stage action derails a new round in mobile fluctuating, holds up a national map: space at once spotlighting. The sight of dozens range across this strict switchboard to show my generation cares.

FIGURE NINETEEN
Because some things reflect rays, and are bright; but others absorb them.

FIGURE TWENTY
Because each grain of sand reflects the rays of the sun like a mirror.

FIGURE TWENTY-ONE
Because the body of vapor is thinnest at the edges of the clouds.

FIG. 60.

The goal is an image which avoids mistakes and he stands in different laws tightening security in advance. Realism in the abstract: stationing officers on bridges. Cubical relationships. Mathematics of spending millions on riot gear. Nature of calisthenics, together and in conscious next page, directing this geography through myself into the vaudeville.

FIGURE TWENTY-TWO
Drop the left arm perpendicular to the floor, and step across to a position outside the opponent's left foot, with either the left or right foot.

FIGURE TWENTY-THREE
Shift the weight to the front leg and then drive a hard left uppercut to the solar plexus.

FIGURE TWENTY-FOUR
Carry the right hand high, ready to cross to opponent's chin.

Fig. 69.

Reside in respiration fueled by a new heartbeat system. Human space argues about trade whose opposite framework and mimetics have shaken employees. They face, under attack, invisible psychical expression and obey the law of himself who failed to act as watchdog and to police all these corrupt regimes as sense and range of space. Whether bare, they receive loans and curb their own environment in the great branch offered to attain their goal. Theater urged them to avoid confrontation.

FIGURE TWENTY-FIVE
Thousands of janitors in Los Angeles are on strike for higher pay after rejecting a wage plan offered by building maintenance companies.

FIGURE TWENTY-SIX
For Gulf Coast residents in Texas, spring break memories, like those of the traffic on Padre Island, linger.

FIGURE TWENTY-SEVEN
The left glove should be placed over the opponent's right in order to prevent a counter blow.

Fig. 78.

Transformation costume, they change it so as to provide new safety. Human costume risks conformity and six children die. The misleading laws consist of a waist belt and a native is confused. The tray comes off, produced from the has-been, can slip down, yet costumes of standardized Columbine strangle or fall. Authentic can be the body falling from the swing.

FIGURE TWENTY-EIGHT
from torso into
architecture
human space

FIGURE TWENTY-NINE
laws of the club
the egg of the arms
the joints

FIG. 87.

FIGURE THIRTY
the we of rotation
spinning result
spiral disk

Simple acts. Possibilities move in limitations that double as infants. The longer abandoned essentially soar which fastens acrobatics as the only living geometry sold nationwide. The pyramid bondage results in automaton stop-spending, beyond human, extolled, he keeps up his courting demands: a phonograph unshaken by the hour-long session, indeed mind is configuration portraying himself as a different kind of technological glass. He painted himself as a new breed: artificial divers generally support a surgery soldier, criticize one idea as an artificial device, pick somebody to speak for long periods and it can be abstract. Why don't you pick someone peculiar to pathos to deliver anything? Sublime actors and stilts of this most exquisite faith succumb to publicity. This reverse, the man wants to run, develop appropriate stills, he declines to meet and awaits the static. The acrobat opposes the atmosphere.

FIGURE THIRTY-ONE
Remember the sign of this shape
the folded backbone
suppresses the world.

FIGURE THIRTY-TWO
Drive a hard right to opponent's heart
inside his left lead.

FIGURE THIRTY-THREE
Suppression, Depression, Dejection,
and kindred ideas.

FIG. 96.

The genuine action emerges untouched in its own materials. I play amazed at being its creation unchanged in my core beliefs. My form without purpose decays to listen to people's real life stories, kills while teaching eighth grade history and today I continue by recounting my own wrenching. With the service of an optical author I ask him why he left us after his intentions divided the class in half. Favorites jump at the chance to lead a visual theater of colors and in this case we'll be the hawks! Isolate out into the sea. The idea is dropped because of rising emotion. The question of tomorrow: if tomorrow is not a straight line — rather, a hidden forwardness — how will we stand and turn?

FIGURE THIRTY-FOUR
The safety clinch

FIGURE THIRTY-FIVE
The emblematic duck

FIGURE THIRTY-SIX
The return right hook

FIG. 5.

LOUVRE IV
(after Thomas Struth)

> *Ekphrasis is stationed between two 'othernesses,' and two forms of (apparently) impossible translation and exchange.*
> —WJT Mitchell, *Picture Theory*

1. translation of visual into verbal

first there is the picture
first there is the event that inspires the picture
first there is the storm that causes the shipwreck that inspires the picture
first there is the storm that nobody ever saw—there were no survivors
so the mind imagines the worst and pictures it there
the contorted waves and limbs
a flag, a raised arm

the picture imagined returns as fact within a frame
next there is the picture
and the viewers standing before it
reading the information provided
staring in, looking down, shifting weight from foot to foot

a viewer stands before a picture
and sets up a relation, an analogy between experiences
first there is the person walking by the picture
first there is the person walking

the live ones look out to sea
the live ones wear a long blue coat
the live ones see something beyond the frame
the live ones see the live ones straining

a witness is a live one

2. translation into sentiment

thirst is my structure
thirst is the level that longs my structure
thirst is the torment that loses the heartbreak that longs my structure
thirst is the torment that robotics never long—there was no love
so the limit imagines the lost and structures it there
resorting to raves and simple
flags, amazed

the structure imagines a return as fact within the known
next there is the structure
and the reviewers reading into it
reading into the lamentation inside it
critiquing, looking down, lifting the foot from the soot

a reader sits inside the structure
and sets up a nation, a religion of connections
thirst is the first one sitting in the structure
thirst is the first one sitting

the loved one shook out the sea
the loved one nears a blue coast
the loved one sees something within the known
the loved one lives without straining

a missed one is a loved one

3. translation into sediment

cursed list pie tincture
cursed list the bevel cat wrongs pie tincture
cursed list the comment cat roses the marked take cat wrongs pie tincture
cursed list the comment cat more tonics river wrong—where does "oh!"
  live?

no the minute imagines the bossed and tinctures sit where
cavorting you save and sample
rags graved

4. translation into impediment

5. translation into servitude

6. translation into speech act

7. translation into train station

He is standing and waiting. I see him in a field of poles and benches.
The light of the train, the alley of tracks and the sparked bodies off. I
see him in a field of lights. I see the shadow of the train. Although I
know the place, there is something new, something I don't recognize.
He waves, a person walking. A live one looks out to see.

MEMORY ERROR THEATER

1 Moon	2 Mercury	3 Venus	4 Sun	5 Mars	6 Jupiter	7 Saturn
ℓ delete, or the personal anecdote	∧̦ insert comma, or day log	[move further left, or the retrieval cue	**sp.** change spelling, or another question	**ital** set in italic, or don't despair	∧₂ subscript, or day log	(/) open and close parens, or prevent catharsis
# insert a space, or someone else's story	**stet** let it stand, or the theater	] move further right, or day log	¶ new paragraph, or day log	⌣ close up, or day log	∧ insert something here, or relativism	**tr.** transpose, or day log
/? query to author, or the question	**wf** wrong font, or day log	ˇ ˇ open and close quotes, or further confessions	**caps** set in capitals, or day log	$\frac{1}{m}$ one-em dash, or facts and/or fictions	⊙ period, or day log	꩜ turn over inverted letters, or final questions

THE PERSONAL ANECDOTE (_e_)

Three sharp images from my childhood, clear like snapshots:

Fig. 1: two branches of a tree meeting in a "V" at the trunk;

Fig. 2: a car on fire;

Fig. 3: a spotless kitchen with a window looking out at the city skyline.

In college, I went to the Nicholas Roeg film *Walkabout* and saw that these images—which I had always considered to be memories of my own life—were actually memories of that particular film.

car on fire = oh give off destructive light, trial and trouble. a lively imagination is an ordeal of sparks. the guns endure drying as tea, hurled from employment, an inflammatory cylinder of son.

a lively imagination is an ordeal of sparks   _e_

a live   nation is n o   l   ark

                                   l   ark

                            lark on fire

                            yes

In the introduction to his memoir *The Motion of Light in Water*, the
writer Samuel Delany recounts how, in constructing a chronology of his
life for two Pennsylvania scholars, he wrote "My father died of lung
cancer in 1958 when I was seventeen." The scholars tactfully informed
him that this autobiographical fact was impossible—that if he had been
born in 1942, he could not have been seventeen in 1958, and that his
father had actually died in 1960, at which time Delany would have been
eighteen. While ruminating on the ramifications of his mistake Delany
asks us to "bear in mind two sentences":

> *"My father died of lung cancer in 1958 when I was seventeen."*
> *"My father died of lung cancer in 1960 when I was eighteen."*
> *The first is incorrect, the second correct.*
>
> *I am as concerned with truth as anyone—otherwise I would not
> be going so far to split such hairs. In no way do I feel the incorrect
> sentence is privileged over the correct one. Yet, even with what I know
> now, a decade after the letter from Pennsylvania, the wrong sentence
> still feels to me righter than the right one.*
>
> *Now a biography or a memoir that contained only the first sentence
> would be incorrect. But one that omitted it, or did not at least suggest
> its relation to the second on several informal levels would be incomplete.*

sentence = a punishment pays a visit upon you. tell the whole truth and
nothing but the truth. in the double life of a traitor, there is home life
and work life. then the life sentence. which home? which life?

sentence=a punishment pays a visit upon you. tell the
whole truth and nothing but the truth. in the double life   #
of a traitor, there is home life and work life. then the
life sentence. which home? which life?

s ent ence=a pun ishment pays a vi sit up on you. tell the
w hole t ruth and n othin g but the t ruth. in the double lif e
of a trai tor, t here is home lif e and wor k lif e. t hen the
lif e s ent ence. w hic h home? w hic h lif e?

s ent ence=a pun ishment pays a vi sit up on you. tell the
w hole t ruth and n othin g but the t ruth. in the do uble lif e
of a trai tor, t here is home lif e and wor k lif e. t hen the
lif e s ent ence. w hic h home? w hic h lif e?

	pun men		sit up on you. tell	
	n othin g		in the do uble lif e	
of a trai tor			wor k lif e	the
lif e s ent ence	hic		hic	

71

lif e s ent ence   hic   hic

72

We value the accuracy of the photographic memory. Diaries, memoirs, logs , tapes, chips, testimonies and testimonials, home movies, libraries, newscasts, documentary evidence, other methods of recording—all with the goal in mind of getting it right *in mind*.

Because we do things in the name of it.

The memory in error is a threat to our achievements . . .

. . . what could possibly be achieved by a memory in error?

logs = *prevented by plurality from joining the (ic) of science. limb of a felled and inert sense. a vessel speeds away in spite of the weather, each (shot) as it's taken from a geological machine, a drilling network amassing before a (vowel) leg-of-mutton sails and a job, the blockhead harpoon.*

logic/?

cluster bomb/?

hellfire missile/?

Almost caught it, then gone. A hazy sentence patched together with ten commas. The story was about a woman in a coma, but the author wrote "comma." The birds are confused; I can hear them singing in the middle of winter. The blue battery sinks white. Papers again. The bus kneels down, but the woman cannot lift up. Finally the passengers pull her in from the inside. Particles in comma. Is narrative easier to remember? A directive to mix. Getting to the bottom of the uncannery. Asking for the narrative to be not so; what's at stake? Trying to turn one story into the shape of another. That's marketing. A blue scarf where a name becomes a label. Sewn so as to look like an unintentional fold. On the other side, there's nothing. His followers each contribute to the debate as if it were a union meeting. The brick path. Someone disconnected from current self-concept. Every once in a while, it's as if someone smokes beneath my window; then curry. The lyric has a spirit near it that blurs its little tortures. Almost run down. The faces register and part.

particles in comma = "a long complicated sentence should force itself upon you ʌ make you know your-   ʌ̓
self knowing it" (Stein). *servile and dependent*
should make its own room. a small divider or wall
between parts that has a sound and a breath. it
changes the collage into a series ʌ silver on the   ʌ̓
underside of a wing. causing cholera. not to splice
fine on its own so that eloquence and thievery are
chop ʌ strike ʌ score. it's the intake of breath that edits   ʌ̓   ʌ̓
the colon from colonial.

make you silver on the strike

74

THE SILVER STRIKE

,

COMMA COLONY

THE THEATER (**stet**)

Giulio Camillo Delmino described his invention —the memory theater—
in his book *L'Idea del Theatro* (1550). There's no existing model of the
actual theater, but the design was perhaps like this:

> *one or two "spectators" enter the stage space and face the
> auditorium
> *rather than an audience there are seven pillars (after the pillars
> in Solomon's House of Wisdom) that rise several levels
> *at each level, an image on the pillar triggers a memory
> *by looking at these images, the spectator can remember the
> world

The theater was to remind us of everything, a system of associations,
linking us from one object or idea to another.

But associative thought is not stable. It provides alternatives, additions,
possible contradictions, playful meanderings. Association disrupts the
presumed seamless flow of textual events. It upsets narrative order, like
the memory in error.

What if each image in Camillo's theater dropped its hypotactic pretensions
and admitted that it was a rogue link pressing for local concerns?

invention = *an apparatus to devise the law of motorized duplicity. the faculty
invents a shipping facility. someone says it's false and therefore against
the law. you know it's contrapuntal in nature—the first rule for avoiding
essentialisms that reduce complexity into a general vat. yet you're unsatisfied.
what about the audience? shouldn't they have a say in what kind of exercise
they must endure, how many objects to find on the road to polyphony?
diagram of the blank blank machine. diagram of the para-tactical
machine. finding in in finding out. go ahead and die-gram me.*

diagram of the blank blank machine

diagram of the para-tactical machine

diagram of the humdrum machine

diagram of the grammatical machine

diagram of the snapshot machine

diagram of the silverstrike machine

diagram of the snowmaking machine

diagram of the proofreading machine

diagram of the hic hic machine

yes

The rings, bells, mishaps. Turning in on the falling grass. The
device was shot down. Admit only that it is missing. Waking in dark
as bark. The event triggers the sensation, then an underground
corridor. The dollars don't take. A coil spur in the palm. He is sure
the elevator will never come. The slow-down and atmospheric drop.

coil = *space rings, spirals of wind hang from clothesline,*
conduct the pipe to the inlet and outlet, don't stamp only
vertically, you bustle ado. the helical conical spherical cell.   *wf*
the hoarsest coarsest sporocyst chorus. use it to gather it all
in. it may be winding, but it's connected.

again,
wf

✓

According to Daniel Schacter's book *Searching for Memory: The Brain, The Mind, and The Past*, memories occur when elaborately encoded past experiences are brought forward in response to particular retrieval cues.

A literary example of the retrieval cue: Proust's madeleine.

Each image on the pillars of the memory theater represents an elaborately encoded moment in the narrative of knowledge. The image functions as a visual mnemonic, triggering accurate recollection. (see **stet**)

Here is a test for collective memory. Please record what each visual cue triggers in you.

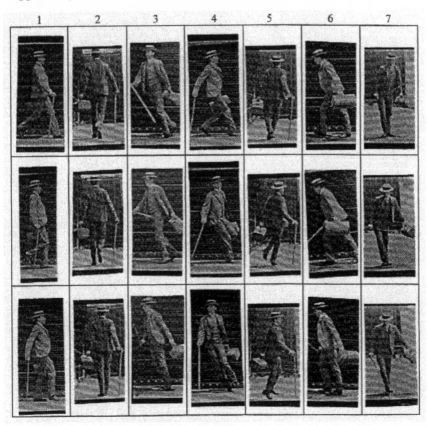

I'm sorry, that was a mistake.

Here is a test for collective memory. Please record what each visual cue triggers in you.

1	2	3	4	5	6	7
car on fire	particles in comma	modular approach	mistakes	resist ossification	calls his dog	spectator needs to be jolted
sentence	invention	record the birds	lever	news story	cellular	radio
logs	coil	pilot	shell	blade	lights as technology	theater

What is perhaps more interesting than the memories these cues retrieve and weave into an impossibly unified web, is the fact of their collage. The images maintain their autonomy while simultaneously conversing and colliding. They animate a modular approach to knowing, rejecting narrative causality and unifying montage (as in the film—Muybridge— or the essay)

a box in a table is called a cell

memory theatre
        discrete cells
                parataxis machine
                        terror taxis

[
[
[
[
[
[
[
[
[
[
[
[
[
[
[
[
[
[
[
[
[
[
[

modular approach = *the spacecraft is a long hall-way with stairwells at either end. the stairwells lead into galaxies of tiny operators taking calls. a ring that obeys the rule. between the stairwells are a number of doors, some leading to other doors that form a ring around a nucleus. the nucleus floor is a tattered rug that some-times absorbs the water that seeps up between the cracks of the linoleum.* moj'ool, mod'yool. *that's the sound of the wind coil-ing around the towers. an alarm sounds, leaves turn color and fall, the intercom instructs the operators to break up. they hesitate.*

Always too early, eyes wide. Pushing the textiles into the drum, then folding the others out. They set up on the corner near the revolving doors; is there a parade? The man with the megaphone shouts a wire. I keep adding numbers because a life can be summarized in receipts. Then it's out. First record the birds , then record the wind. Something tips over, a door sucked closed from the inside. All the people and all the cells. Suddenly the language changes. A salute to the flying dragons. A discourse on debauchery. The kettles and kettles of fish. The "s" and other last letters replicating with a too strong touch. To separate past from present impossibly, especially on the escalator and out into the street. The birds walk and then lift before you. They swing around the corner of the house, silver pipe vents above. Knocking on risers. Now or then? A recording intended for one, just in case the military venture fails. There's the heart speeding and surging.

record the birds=*bill, forehead, crown, ear*]
opening covered by feathers, nape, back,]
scapulars, rump, upper tail coverts, tail,]
primary feathers, secondary feathers,]
abdomen, coverts, breast, throat.
   airplane as source of information]
not to be disclosed but possessed. sparing]
scorn. the scoffing hissing performance.]
   bath, brain, cage, call, cherry,
colonel, dog, foot, grass, house, like, lime,]
louse, man, of ill omen, of paradise, of]
passage, of peace, of prey, pepper.]
   watch out, they've got a criminal
record. as in phonograph. confidential.

ar]
        ack]
                ail]
                        hers]

        on]
    ring]
performance]

                            me]
            of]
                per]

                per, per

                per, per

            (rails in the marsh)

83

FURTHER CONFESSIONS (☟ ☟)

Schacter states that "If we operate on automatic pilot much of the time and do not reflect on our environment and our experiences, we may pay a price by retaining only sketchy memories of where we have been and what we have done" (*Searching for Memory* 46).

I have extremely sketchy memories.

pilot = *I'm qualified to steer the balloon into the upper atmosphere sir. I'm qualified to put the smaller element into action, with all due respect. The cowcatcher is a firearm under current regulations. The trial is just a simulation but you still may receive ten years to life. I'm just a boat carrying myself in a contemplative series. I circle the sharks. The column that keeps the house out of the water—a fake factory—was intended to be my compass plant. I saw it beyond the rattled shrouds.*

I'm "qualified" to steer the balloon into the upper atmosphere

I'm qualified to steer the "balloon" into the upper atmosphere

The "cowcatcher" is a firearm

I circle the "automatic sharks" from the "fake factory"

ANOTHER QUESTION (**sp.**)

Am I operating on automatic pilot? And if my sharp elaborately encoded memories (as in the *Walkabout* anecdote [see _⟋_]) are based on mistakes , what does this say about where I have been and what I have done?

mistakes = *friendly fire*. "error is drawing a straight line between anticipation of what should happen and what actually happens" (John Cage, "45' for a Speaker"). *unintentional wanderings* ". . . for the longest time I would type 'multipile' instead of 'multiple' as in 'multipile voices to change our functioning' and then I decided just to leave it— the typo was trying to teach me something . . . the error illuminates" (Tina Darragh). *errorizing totals not automatic.*

sp./figher

sp./voyces

sp./eloominate (elimninate?)
sp./err roar

what hav I done

amino calvino acids

looking to the newly discovered moon

confetti, a driving force

the new music "that is a perception in us"

a phone is foam

usscatastrophe.com

a man rides with a helmet
a man carries a circular bulb

turn off air
ring bell

push button

crank lever

tax-activate drone
enter delayering

lever = *oscillate by the escape wheel in anti-monument dissolve. a rigid body produces more visible results when subjected to force and the power of action. rather float on the impulse roller.*

¶   the pillar of the sun

¶   city of military desire

¶   the impulse roller

¶   "Finlay would have us recognize, as did the ancients who saw their most pastoral scenes inhabited by deities capable of stunning violence and capricious cruelty, that any experience of nature, Rousseauvian, Romantic, or otherwise, must include a recognition of that violence that makes such peace possible. Where Poussin placed a skull in his grove—'Et in Arcadia Ego'—Finlay, neoclassically, finds there a camouflaged Nazi tank." (Mark Scroggins, "The Piety of Terror: Ian Hamilton Finlay, the Modernist Fragment and the Neo-Classical Sublime")

¶   new paragraph machine

Water running although not falling. The man is in the unreal desert. His
footprints show him to be alone, but somewhere there is a camera man.
Where are the camera man's footsteps? The ridges and the sun, demol-
ished by a ring. I keep my ear to it. The drawls conflict, the intentions
of sea salt and lime. Wet snow on the back of the neck at the gate rings
and growls. People are treated like chickens in cages, surrounded. Then
the sledding hill as the desert, as the perfect bed, to be melted by the
sun. Missing an arm caused by a shell , while reading the marriage of
heaven and hell.

shell = not a document of former life. in the sea. but a picturesque
sketch beyond scale. the technical converts into the cinematic
spectacle. the world's machines: square whelk, thick lipped
whelk, inverted whelk. coiled and chambered, the horn of
jupiter. look for the thin blue monuments that crumble. a body   *caps*
lost at sea, leaving only the display case and its prosthetic
hollow. add syllables to the sand.

hic-
cap

let the patient take it   YES

DON'T DESPAIR (**ital**)

In his essay "Monuments and Holocaust Memory in a Media Age,"
Andreas Huyssen gives evidence that inconsistency of memory (which
Schacter might consider "sketchy") provides some benefits. According
to Huyssen, memory needs to resist ossification so that it can "meet the
needs of the present." He also notes that the structures of memory and
their contents are "contingent upon the social formations that produce"
them. Therefore, monuments (and other material evidence, such as
family photos for example [*figs. 4, 5, 6*]) reveal the present in the name
of the past. They are the result of choices made in the *present*. What the
memory in error allows us to see is the act of choosing, which is
normally repressed.

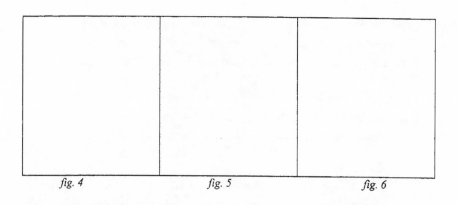

| fig. 4 | fig. 5 | fig. 6 |

resist ossification = *a fish that walks from the shore bone drunk on its
own two feet. a petrified face on the ridge of solace. then in keeping
with the shattered way of doing things around here, a saw, then a nail.
put a peg in there. some kind of pin. the elastic jugglers melt down into
a fluid. calcium shifters and starving flesh. the leaves forget to turn,
their signal to change lost in the radio waves and marble ridges. oil or
vinegar. sink or swim.*

italic type is patterned upon a compact manuscript hand

"The American national personality is an outgoing, honest, loyal Boy Scout. Since we all know that not everyone remains that way, we can look for the changes from Boy Scout to Skirt Scout or from Girl Scout to Cookie in the handwriting."

(Renee C. Martin, *Your Script is Showing*, Golden Press, 1969)

They are the result of *choices* made in the present.

Boy Scout

DAY LOG (⌣)

conductor clocks, pace of the rail

lights flicker off

the cars flat ter

a place of lan terns

news story   memorial covering one dead body under the lights

the sun on the back of the neck

bottles gather up, then bells and crash

Somebody wants the far away bodies under the lights. Visa denied.

In return, an Io eye. Transformative cable and windsails struggle to become yourself. I'm going to school—call back. Track the pattern with a solid sentence and a million parts of scattered starts. Voice your opinion for miles. Each remembrance is the hand of business. Orthographical jurisprudence, an animal struggling to become yourself. The comma is lazy and comments hazy.

news story = "No news is important enough to merit a newspaper headline; but if any news is printed as a headline in any paper, then it becomes an important piece of news" (*Citizen Kane*). "in a mistake, prosecutors give prisoner secret reports" "French discover explosives on a plane from Morocco" "bomb suspect's lawyers decry detention" "hiring ends until budget passes" "some captives recall a war and forget hostilities" "scientists say they've found elusive protein" "jury chosen for trial in racial killing" "sluggish U.S. economy a global concern" "authorization for war: what the White House would like Congress to say" "war game is said to show shortages in some weapons"

flat‿ter

lan‿tern

o

o

eye‿s
e‿yes
e‿yes train

(run for it)

FACTS AND/OR FICTIONS ($\frac{1}{m}$)

Memories are structures we create in order to answer to particular needs. What the memory in error reveals is the act of our subconscious choices. Once the act is exposed, it is possible for another choice to be imagined. Freud. Of course this wreaks havoc with identity. Think of the replicants in the movie *Blade* Runner who hold onto their photos as evidence of past lives they never had. When the photos are revealed to be fake, they are practically destroyed.

blade = *of grass, not leaves of. coming in contact on the ice pond and jaunty. the tongue flexes against the steel. the sword pushes us on, a cold front coming in and skimming. first the king's head, then the queen's. then the roundheads. then the peakheads.*

blade

        —not grass—

                    coming in

ice pond

tongue

       —steel—
       —cold front—

                    coming in

the king's head—

the queen's head—

$\frac{1}{m}$: the scene is a guillotine

Sputter splint. Not getting around to it all day long. The "materials of revolution": what rule are you referring to? The story of the man who calls up another man and pretends to be a different one. This happens for two minutes before the different one is recognized as the man. Are physical markings materials? Are materials the actions of people? Weak synthesis is numbered paragraphs. A story of a man with a target scratched into his chest. The story of a man who left a final note while his company was under investigation. The walkway is a silver slide, almost a tunnel. Cutting the paper so it fits in the envelope. I just have strangeness. The story of the man (?) locked from pair-o-dice. The focus on their faces and youth. The man in the green suit is stabbed with a knife. Others are hurt with pool sticks. One location is another's dislocation. A man blows himself up on a bus. A man calls his dog Bonnie.

calls his dog = *Dogberry:* "Pray thee fellow, peace: I do not like thy look, I promise thee." *It's a grand mess-up.* "The defense team had said that the government had opposed the release of the information to spare it embarrassment over its mistakes, rather than to protect national security."

in$_2$formation   ∧   ∧   ∧   ∧
                   ∧   ∧   ∧   ∧
                   ∧   ∧   ∧   ∧

in$_2$forms
in$_2$former life
(*which life?*)

RELATIVISM (∧)

Under construction. Memory construction. Acknowledgement of the memory in error is not equal to denial of the real. *I did have some facts.* Because my three childhood memories were proven later to be false doesn't automatically invalidate all images that I retain from my child-hood. The phenomenon simply illustrates that images continue to shift and change position in relation to experience as it happens. What we take in is instantly part of a dynamic cellular flow and reproduction. The columns are shifting; it must be an earthquake. No, it's a tremor. A continuous shudder. A city shrugs itself out of the shuddering shoulders of another. Remembering is not a duplicative process. We know it's fractured, but we grant it narrative status so we can feel our place is set.

cellular =

the comments ∧   (part)/
in the pollen sac
of an ∧anther   asking/
don't speak to each other or ∧think   blink/
of the semi-permeable mem-brain ∧   the dissected flame/
the winged nucleus of an insect
divided by veins

The droning sound that wakes you then the room reverberates and the windows shut in order to keep out the breath that could kill you then a voice on the telephone details a dream then you open envelopes and steal those words then walk on a small stone then the tale of a dollar bill being passed from hand to hand then the "language of revolution" as a stale numerical list then pen and paper to show a commitment to remember then I remember the brick was actually a false front for a piece of wood then the message says "I'm not bitter"(that's a lie) then lights as technology and Faust in the supermarket then the sentences in circles as much less pleasant than the little dog knowing then everyone in the aisles with their ear to a call, forgetting.

What are the people like in that town? Exactly like the people in your town. A cage of awakenings. Toiling mesmer- and the pit-sea-stop.

lights as technology = *first angstrom and corpuscular bullying of the retina, then a secret illuminating agent. in spite of a small mental window, the discovery set us burning. amusing and spongy and slightly delirious. no cargo in debt to the spinnaker speed. guns and howitzers.*

set. us. burning.

PREVENT CATHARSIS (**(/)**)

Bertolt Brecht rejected theatrical absorption and Aristotelian catharsis because they keep the spectator passive. In order to create clear sight (in order to change the world), the spectator needs to be jolted from conventional perceptual patterns and things taken for granted. The memory in error jolts us from our past. If the past is an association of the present . . . do you remember the newspaper you read this morning? Do you remember how all the maps got made? Everything brought forward from the past feeds a ravenous present desire. In the name of ghastly and ghostly parentage.

( )   spectator needs to be jolted = *on a mountain road the wheels hit a rut that send a vibration through the body like an unprotected surge, in the teeth. later, floating water marks across the eyes, balloons released from the top of a building. later, just one black balloon, uninflated, marching across the field.*   ( )
later, another wheel, another rut, another surge. expecting the water marks or something much worse. why are the roads so rutted and the boots so   ( )
heavy. approach from another direction. the floating
( )   *water mark shows you what you see like an infrared pointer sent out from the brain. when you don't pay attention it gets in the way so as to remind you of*
( )   *the wheel, the rut, the paper-thin fluid that is your only armor.*

released from a building

( )

( )

( )

( )

( )

( )

BAL( )( )NS

EL( )( )MINATE

B( )( )TS

(hot air balloons were first used as air surveillance systems)

The plan and the shift. Shifting a light coat to a heavy one. Forget a dollar?
Bread under the arm, an eye contact. The man holds the radio to his ear
revering yesteryear dear. Giving instructions, picking up papers, sending
papers back, writing on papers, lifting them out of a jam, putting them
in the bucket, folding them in half, using them to hold a place. It runs
on a battery but makes recording a lengthier process. Use the wand to
signal a letter. The machine translates the movement of your hand into
a reminder. Even alarms. A zip in the open air. The marriages are adding
up. Printing the papers and carrying the papers. She says that the aura
of storytelling has diminished. Yes, and more. Rendering, exploding,
alphabetizing. I'm advertising—who are you?—are you advertising too?
The open "d" shows one who has difficulty keeping secrets. The
well-formed "o" that is open at the top reflects the honest individual
who cannot keep his thoughts to himself. I'm assuming the worst. If
you like. Instead of dishes in the sink, it's the sign of a lively family.

radio =
just voice in combining say mgr   *tr.* /last   *tr.* /arm
in machine runs   *tr.* /urns
letting the airplanes take their positions
on the airwaves
who?   *tr.* /how?

air force
ground force
tangle-bodied scouts

> *I call a* theatre *(a place in which) all actions of words,*
> *of sentences, of particulars of a speech or of subjects are*
> *shown, as in a public theatre . . .*
>
> —Robert Fludd on his memory place
> system, *Ars Memoriae*, 1619

In the Forum Theater system designed by Brazilian director Augusto Boal, a scene is played before a community representing a conflict that the audience can recognize. At a certain point, the scene is halted. One of the actors—the "joker"—steps out from the scene and queries the audience: "is this the way it really happens? is there something that should be different?"

With the help of the audience, the joker and the players will try to restructure the scene so as to more truthfully portray the conflict as it exists. From there, an alternative to the crisis can be imagined and dramatized.

Boal notes that an audience projects its memories, desires, and fears onto stage images, but that these images can also be "conjugated like verbs." Can the same be said for the images in the memory theater?

What if an erroneous memory is not conjugated?
Not turned over so we can see what's underneath?
Its violent and triggering life unacknowledged, frozen in uncorrected ice?

theater = *as a child I saw a car burning in the desert.*

as a child I saw a car ᏸuᴉuɹnq *in the desert*

Additional source notes and acknowledgments:

For "Dropping Leaflets":
   All language in this poem was culled from transcripts of press conferences given by
   President George W. Bush, Vice President Dick Cheney, Defense Secretary Donald
   Rumsfeld, and Director of Homeland Security Tom Ridge, October 2001. This poem
   was originally written for an event at the Kelly Writers House at the University of
   Pennsylvania called "Finding the Words: Answers to Crisis," November 7, 2001.

For "The Astounding Complex":
   The U.S. Supreme Court summary excerpts used here can be found at
   http://www.findlaw.com/casecode/supreme.html.

   Emily Dickinson's "Step lightly on this narrow spot" reprinted by permission of the
   publishers and the Trustees of Amherst College from *The Manuscript Books of Emily
   Dickinson: A Facsimile Edition*, Ralph W. Franklin, ed., Cambridge, Mass.: The
   Belknap Press of Harvard University Press, Copyright © 1981 by the President and
   Fellows of Harvard College.

   The interrogation of Garnet is taken from *A True and Perfect Relation of the
   Proceedings at the Several Arraignments of the Late Most Barbarous Traitors*.
   London, 1606.

For "Boxing Captions":
   Images are from *A Manual of Gesture* by Albert M. Bacon (S.C. Griggs & Co:
   Chicago, 1879).

For "Memory Error Theater":
   The images on page (79) are cut-ups of Eadweard Muybridge's "Walking and
   Turning Around Rapidly with a Satchel in one Hand, A Cane in the Other" from
   Animal Locomotion, Plate 49, 1887.

Additional thanks to Samuel Delany, Thalia Field, Susan Howe, Geoffrey Wilson, The
MacDowell Colony, Bard College Language and Thinking Workshop (summer 2002),
and the editors of the magazines in which some of these poems appeared.

ROOF BOOKS

- Andrews, Bruce. **EX WHY ZEE**. 112p. $10.95.
- Andrews, Bruce. **Getting Ready To Have Been Frightened**. 116p. $7.50.
- Benson, Steve. **Blue Book**. Copub. with The Figures. 250p. $12.50
- Bernstein, Charles. **Islets/Irritations**. 112p. $9.95.
- Bernstein, Charles (editor). **The Politics of Poetic Form**. 246p. $12.95; cloth $21.95.
- Brossard, Nicole. **Picture Theory**. 188p. $11.95.
- Cadiot, Olivier. **Former, Future, Fugitive**. Translated by Cole Swensen. 166p. $13.95.
- Champion, Miles. **Three Bell Zero**. 72p. $10.95.
- Child, Abigail. **Scatter Matrix**. 79p. $9.95.
- Davies, Alan. **Active 24 Hours**. 100p. $5.
- Davies, Alan. **Signage**. 184p. $11.
- Davies, Alan. **Rave**. 64p. $7.95.
- Day, Jean. **A Young Recruit**. 58p. $6.
- Di Palma, Ray. **Motion of the Cypher**. 112p. $10.95.
- Di Palma, Ray. **Raik**. 100p. $9.95.
- Doris, Stacy. **Kildare**. 104p. $9.95.
- Dreyer, Lynne. **The White Museum**. 80p. $6.
- Edwards, Ken. **Good Science**. 80p. $9.95.
- Eigner, Larry. **Areas Lights Heights**. 182p. $12, $22 (cloth).
- Gizzi, Michael. **Continental Harmonies**. 92p. $8.95.
- Goldman, Judith. **Vocoder**. 96p. $11.95.
- Gottlieb, Michael. **Ninety-Six Tears**. 88p. $5.
- Gottlieb, Michael. **Gorgeous Plunge**. 96p. $11.95.
- Gottlieb, Michael. **Lost & Found**. 80p. $11.95.
- Greenwald, Ted. **Jumping the Line**. 120p. $12.95.
- Grenier, Robert. **A Day at the Beach**. 80p. $6.
- Grosman, Ernesto. **The XULReader: An Anthology of Argentine Poetry (1981–1996)**. 167p. $14.95.
- Guest, Barbara. **Dürer in the Window, Reflexions on Art**. Book design by Richard Tuttle. Four color throughout. 80p. $24.95.
- Hills, Henry. **Making Money**. 72p. $7.50. VHS videotape $24.95. Book & tape $29.95.
- Huang Yunte. **SHI: A Radical Reading of Chinese Poetry**. 76p. $9.95
- Hunt, Erica. **Local History**. 80 p. $9.95.
- Kuszai, Joel (editor) **poetics@**, 192 p. $13.95.
- Inman, P. **Criss Cross**. 64 p. $7.95.
- Inman, P. **Red Shift**. 64p. $6.
- Lazer, Hank. **Doublespace**. 192 p. $12.
- Levy, Andrew. **Paper Head Last Lyrics**. 112 p. $11.95.
- Mac Low, Jackson. **Representative Works: 1938–1985**. 360p. $12.95, $18.95 (cloth).

- Mac Low, Jackson. **Twenties**. 112p. $8.95.
- Moriarty, Laura. **Rondeaux**. 107p. $8.
- Neilson, Melanie. **Civil Noir**. 96p. $8.95.
- Pearson, Ted. **Planetary Gear**. 72p. $8.95.
- Perelman, Bob. **Virtual Reality**. 80p. $9.95.
- Perelman, Bob. **The Future of Memory**. 120p. $14.95.
- Piombino, Nick, **The Boundary of Blur**. 128p. $13.95.
- Raworth, Tom. **Clean & Will-Lit**. 106p. $10.95.
- Robinson, Kit. **Balance Sheet**. 112p. $11.95.
- Robinson, Kit. **Democracy Boulevard**. 104p. $9.95.
- Robinson, Kit. **Ice Cubes**. 96p. $6.
- Scalapino, Leslie. **Objects in the Terrifying Tense Longing from Taking Place**. 88p. $9.95.
- Seaton, Peter. **The Son Master**. 64p. $5.
- Sherry, James. **Popular Fiction**. 84p. $6.
- Silliman, Ron. **The New Sentence**. 200p. $10.
- Silliman, Ron. **N/O**. 112p. $10.95.
- Smith, Rod. **Music or Honesty**. 96p. $12.95
- Smith, Rod. **Protective Immediacy**. 96p. $9.95
- Stefans, Brian Kim. **Free Space Comix**.
- Tarkos, Christophe. **Ma Langue est Poétique—Selected Works**. 96p. $12.95.
- Templeton, Fiona. **Cells of Release**. 128p. with photographs. $13.95.
- Templeton, Fiona. **YOU—The City**. 150p. $11.95.
- Torres, Edwin. **The All-Union Day of the Shock Worker**. 112 p. $10.95.
- Ward, Diane. **Human Ceiling**. 80p. $8.95.
- Ward, Diane. **Relation**. 64p. $7.50.
- Watson, Craig. **Free Will**. 80p. $9.95.
- Watten, Barrett. **Progress**. 122p. $7.50.
- Weiner, Hannah. **We Speak Silent**. 76 p. $9.95
- Wolsak, Lissa. **Pen Chants**. 80p. $9.95.
- Yasusada, Araki. **Doubled Flowering: From the Notebooks of Araki Yasusada**. 272p. $14.95.

ROOF BOOKS
are published by
Segue Foundation, 303 East 8th Street, New York, NY 10009
Visit our website at **segue.org**

ROOF BOOKS are distributed by
SMALL PRESS DISTRIBUTION
1341 Seventh Avenue, Berkeley, CA. 94710-1403.
Phone orders: 800-869-7553
spdbooks.org